The Spectrum No One Sees

An Autistic Woman's Voice:
Poetry and short stories on Motherhood, Mental Health, and Identity

Author: Karla Luciana Chinen

THE SPECTRUM NO ONE SEES

An Autistic Woman's Voice: Poetry on Motherhood, Mental Health, and Identity

Copyright © 2026 by **Karla Luciana Chinen**

All rights reserved.

No part of this publication may be reproduced, stored in a retrieval system, or transmitted in any form or by any means—electronic, mechanical, photocopying, recording, or otherwise—without prior written permission of the author, except in the case of brief quotations used in reviews, articles, or educational commentary.

This book is a work of creative expression.

Names, details, and personal experiences are presented from the author's perspective.

Any resemblance to actual persons, living or dead, is coincidental unless explicitly noted by the author.

Cover art and interior design by **Karla Luciana Chinen**

Published by **[your publishing name or Empathy for Autism California]**

Printed in the United States of America

ISBN: 979-8-218-91452-3 and 979-8-218-91453-0

For permissions and inquiries, please contact:
Karla@empathyforautismcalifornia.com

First Edition: 2026

Dedication

For my children —

my mirrors, my teachers, my softest truth.

For the child I once was —

I will never silence you again.

For every mother raising autistic children —

your voice matters,

your storms matter,

you matter.

Prologue

There is a private landscape inside me,

rich with color and quiet,

full of thoughts that move in ways

the outside world cannot measure.

I move through life with steady hands

while my inner life shifts and reshapes itself

like a living canvas of emotion and sensation.

I am an autistic woman raising autistic children.

Their experiences open doors to memories

I once locked away,

and they teach me to view myself

with more compassion than I ever received.

This book offers a glimpse into that inner terrain.

Not to explain or defend,

but to illuminate the depth,

the beauty,

and the truth

of a mind that simply moves differently.

This is the spectrum no one sees.

Dedication	5
Prologue	7
Chapter 1: A Mind Made of Thunder	16
The Room Behind My Eyes	16
The Day I Learned to Pretend	17
Electric Skin	18
The Question I Never Knew How to Answer	19
Script	20
Blue Tile Floor	21
When Thoughts Refuse to Rest	22
The Library in My Chest	23
Glass House	24
Naming	25
Chapter 2: Motherhood in the Quiet Hours	26
The Lineage of Women	26
Thread	28
The Shape of Love	28
First Time I Saw My Daughter Break	29
My Grandmother's Kitchen	31
The Night I Crossed Into a New Life	34
When I Became the Safe Space I Needed	38

Instructions for a Mexican Daughter	40
My Other Grandmother's Hands	41
Motherhood Without a Map	43
My Mother's Shadow and My Own Light	44
The Instructions My Culture Forgot to Give	46
When My Daughter Looked at Me Differently	47
The Thread That Did Not Break	49
Becoming the First Woman in	50
My Line to Rest	50
Chapter 3: The Girl Who Mirrors My Sky	53
When I Saw Myself in Her Eyes	53
The Day She Heard What Others Missed	54
Lines of Light	55
The Moment She Realized I Understand Her	56
Seed of Strength	57
Her Sensitivity Is Her Superpower	58
The Way She Studies the World	59
The Language Between Us	60
When She Reminds Me of the Girl I Was	61
She Is Not Afraid of Her Voice	62
Daughter of Insight	63

The Quiet Thread Between Us	64
When She Walks Into the Room	68
The Daughter Who Teaches Me Light	70

Chapter 4: The Boy Made of Constellations — 73

The First Time I Held a Universe	73
The Boy Who Speaks in Echoes of Dawn	74
He Carries Fire and Softness Together	75
When He Looks Into My Eyes	76
Storm and Sanctuary	77
His Strength Does Not Announce Itself	78
The Weightless Moments	79
The Touch That Speaks More Than Words	80
The Mirror That Shows Me Truth	81
The World He Builds Inside Himself	82
The Boy Who Walks Between Stars	83
Moonbinder	84
The Night He Reached for the Sky	85
Moon Language	86
He Walks the Edge of Hidden Worlds	87
When His Hands Tremble,	90
I Become the Earth Beneath Him	90

The Boy Who Borrowed the Song	93
The Shadow He Takes My Hand Through	96
Chapter 5: The Inner Landscape	101
The Architecture of My Mind	101
When the World Feels Too Loud	102
The Mask I Learned to Wear	103
When Silence Becomes Language	104
The Sensory Thread	105
The Truth I No Longer Hide	106
How I Learned to Stay	108
The Day I Owned My Name	109
Becoming the Change	110
The Center of the Constellation	111
The Hour the Air Turns Heavy	112
The House With the Locked Staircase	115
Chapter 6: The Woman Who Did Not Break	122
The Rooms I Built Myself	122
The Weight I Learned to Carry Without Breaking	126
The Spine Made of Fire	128
The Day I Chose Myself	129
The Man Who Matched My Silence	131

When Two Unusual Souls Choose Each Other	134
When Two Shadows Found the Same Light	137
The Gravity Between Us	139
The Strange Belongs to Us	141

Chapter 7: The Mind That Learns, Remembers, and Rises — 143

The Mind That Refuses to Sleep	143
The Invisible Thread of Intuition	144
The Comfort I Built With My Own Hands	145
When Grief Arrived Too Early	146
The Brother I Protected	148
The Art of Pretending I Understood	149
Social Rules	149
The Woman I Am in My Work	151
The Night the House Would Not Sleep	152
The Last Afternoon with My Grandfather	154
The Day my Father Tried in His Own Way	155
The Hallway Between my Brother and Me	156
The Room Where I Finally Stepped into My Voice	157
The Night Windows of My Mind	158
Prayer Without a Name	158

The Bear on the Bed	159
Grandfather's Conversations	160
From the Girl I Was	163
My Father Learning How to Say My Name	165
Five Years and a Hallway	165
In Rooms Full of Small Talk	166
When I Step onto the Stage	166
Blessing for the Men Who Stayed Kind	167
Santa Bob: The Man Who Arrived Like A Season	168
Maria	172
Closing Spell for My Own Heart	176
The Woman Whose Love Holds the Walls Steady	177
The Woman they Called Cabrona	179
In Praise of The Cabrona	183
Lita and Abu	185
Chapter 8: Final Thoughts	188
The Last Ember	188
The Bridge I Did Not Know I Was Building	191
A Thank You to the Ones Like Me	195
About the Author	198

Chapter 1: A Mind Made of Thunder

The Room Behind My Eyes

There is a room behind my eyes
that shifts shape
depending on the day.
Some mornings it glows
like warm glass.
Other mornings
it is a dim hallway
lined with thoughts
that refuse to move.
This room belongs to me,
whether the world understands it or not.
Here, my reactions are not dramatic.
They make perfect sense.

The Day I Learned to Pretend

I was six the first time I realized
that the world expected me
to behave differently
than I felt.
The classroom buzzed with movement.
Chairs scraped.
Voices stacked on top of each other.
A pencil shattered on the floor.
Every sound struck me like a spark.
But everyone else continued
as if nothing had happened.
I put my head down.
The teacher frowned.
A few kids giggled.
So I put my head up.
My body still flinched,
but I kept my face still.
That was the moment I understood
that pretending made adults relax.
So I pretended.

Electric Skin

My senses do not sit quietly.
They surge.
They pull.
They react.
A soft sound can feel sharp.
A bright light can feel physical.
My skin absorbs details
long before my mind decides
what to do with them.
By evening
my nerves feel scraped,
as if the day has worn them thin.
People believe I am distant.
I am not.
I am protecting myself
from everything I cannot turn off.

The Question I Never Knew How to Answer

People often asked,
"Why do you zone out?"
I never knew how to answer
without telling the entire truth.
Because I am overstimulated.
Because I am thinking of twenty things at once.
Because I am watching every expression in the room.
Because I do not want to misread your tone.
Because speaking takes energy I do not always have.
Instead I said,
"I am fine. I am listening."
It was easier
than explaining a language
no one else spoke.

Script

Before walking into a room
I rehearse.
Hello.
How are you.
I am good.
Thank you.
I adjust my face
like someone arranging flowers.
I place the smile just right
so no one notices
how much effort it takes.
Later I return home
and realize
I did not speak as myself
even once.

Blue Tile Floor

I remember the mercado
with a floor of blue tiles
smells that took my mind to different places.
I was an adult,
but the sensory overload
made me feel five again.
Voices echoed.
crates clattered.
Someone's perfume
hung in the air too strong.
My heart beat fast.
I tried to breathe slow.
A woman asked if I needed help.
I shook my head.
Words were too slippery
to hold.
I stood still for a moment
until I could find myself again.
No one saw the panic
because I had learned
to hold it quietly.

When Thoughts Refuse to Rest

My thoughts rarely move in straight lines.
They bend like rivers
that refuse to follow the map.
Night brings silence,
but not peace.
I lie in the dark
and watch memories return,
persistent and bright,
as if they never aged.
People say let it go.
If only the mind obeyed
commands.

The Library in My Chest

Inside me lives a library
of moments I never chose to keep.
Not the joyful ones.
Those fade softly.
It is the sharp ones
that stay loud.
A careless word.
A raised volume.
A misunderstanding
that left a mark.
They sit on shelves
waiting for the quiet,
when my guard is down,
so they can step forward again.
I do not revisit them
because I want to.
They revisit me
because they can.

Glass House

I live with feelings that break easily
because they feel deeply.
I walk through conversations
as if the floor might crack.
Others throw their words freely.
They are safe in stone houses.
I have always lived in glass.

Naming

When I finally learned the word autistic
I did not feel fear.
I felt recognition.
A map unfolded.
The pieces aligned.
The questions had context.
It was not a sentence.
It was clarity.
The name did not change me.
It explained me.

Chapter 2: Motherhood in the Quiet Hours

The Lineage of Women

My motherhood began long before I held my own children.
It began in the stories of the women who came before me.
My grandmother rose before the sun every day of her life.
She carried water in her hands, faith in her chest, and pain in her silence.
Her softness was not gentle.
It was labor.
It was survival dressed as obedience.
My other grandmother lived in shadows of expectation,
where a woman could not speak too loudly or dream too boldly
without being punished for wanting more than her chores.
She learned to swallow grief whole.
She learned to smile with her eyes lowered.
Then there was my mother,
who crossed a border while carrying my brother in her belly,
walking into a country that did not want her
and a life that demanded more than any one person should give.

She worked in houses that were not hers,
cleaning floors while trying to keep her own life from collapsing.
She held bruises on the inside,
quiet ones that came from exhaustion, fear, and never being enough
for a world that expected perfection from a woman with no support.
I watched her push through storms with a face of stone
and a spine that refused to bend.
She never cried in front of us.
She never stopped moving.
She never allowed herself to fall apart.
And somewhere in all of that,
I learned that motherhood was sacrifice.
Not choice, but duty.
Not softness, but endurance.
Not gentleness, but survival.
When I became a mother myself,
I realized I had inherited not only their strength
but also their wounds.

Thread

I carry the thread
of every woman before me.
Some threads are gold.
Some are frayed.
Some cut my fingers when I hold them.
But I braid them anyway
because they are mine,
and because my daughter and son
deserve a softer fabric
than the one I was wrapped in.

The Shape of Love

Love is not gentle for me.
It expands too quickly.
It overwhelms my senses.
But when it comes to my children,
love is a shape I grow into
no matter how heavy it becomes.

First Time I Saw My Daughter Break

She was only five when I saw the trembling in her hands.
A sound in the room had shifted,
something sharp, something sudden,
and her whole body went stiff
the way mine still does.
Her eyes filled fast,
not with tears but with confusion,
as if her skin no longer belonged to her.
I recognized that feeling.
I had lived my entire childhood inside it.
I knelt beside her without speaking.
Words would have made the moment worse.
I simply placed my hand near hers,
not touching, just close enough
so she felt she was not alone.
She curled toward me,
tiny and shaking,
her breath broken into pieces.
And I understood then
that I was raising a child
who would inherit not only my love
but also my struggles.

In that moment I promised her something
no one had ever promised me,
that she would never have to navigate that feeling alone.

My Grandmother's Kitchen

I learned the meaning of womanhood in my
grandmother's Mexican kitchen, a place where the walls held
more secrets than photographs.
The stove was always warm.
A pot of beans simmered quietly in the corner.
Homemade tortillas rested under a cloth that smelled like
the sun.
And on the table stood a bowl of chiles so bright and fiery
they felt like a warning disguised as food.
My grandmother moved through that kitchen
as if it were both sanctuary and prison.
Her hands carried the memory of field work,
of cooking for rich people, of sewing late into the night just to
keep the lights on.
She never complained.
Mexican women did not complain.
They endured.
They swallowed grief like caldo.
They carried stress in their backs
and called it "life."

They accepted silence as a duty,
not a choice.
She woke before sunrise
and slept last, her body a servant to everyone else's needs
before her own.
I watched her suffer quietly under the weight of cultural
expectations that told her she must be strong,
but also obedient, soft-spoken, humble,
and grateful even when the world gave her so little.
She never showed fear.
She never showed weakness.
She never showed herself.
Her silence was not a personality.
It was survival.
Her generation of women carried trauma
with the same familiarity
as carrying groceries home from the mercado.
They were taught to stay
even when their hearts wanted to leave.
They were taught to forgive
even when they were never forgiven.
They were taught to serve
even when they were exhausted.
Mexican culture celebrates women who endure.
It rarely celebrates women who rest.
And then there is me.

An autistic woman
who feels deeply,
who questions everything,
who refuses to disappear into silence
the way the women before me had to.
When my daughter sits across from me in the kitchen,
legs dangling off a chair too big for her,
I open my mouth
and speak the words my grandmother could not:
It is okay to cry.
It is okay to be overwhelmed.
It is okay to feel everything.
It is okay to rest.
It is okay to say no.
It is okay to be loud.
It is okay to protect your spirit.
My grandmother's kitchen taught me how women survive.
I am teaching my daughter how women heal.

The Night I Crossed Into a New Life

I was four years old the night my life split into a before
and an after.
My mother held my hand in one palm and her swollen belly
in the other,
eight months pregnant and moving through the desert
as if fear itself were pushing her forward.
The cold surprised me.
I had never known that sand could freeze under your feet.
My mother dressed me in a snow suit that made my arms
stiff and my legs heavy.
The hood framed my face so tightly
I could hear my own breath echo back at me.
I held on to my teddy bear the entire time,
pressing its worn fur against my cheek
whenever the wind grew too sharp.
He was the only softness in a night that felt made of stone.
Each step buried my boots in the sand.
I had to pull my feet out with effort,
the grains sliding around my ankles

like cold hands trying to hold me in place.
My mother did not let go of me.
Her grip tightened every time someone whispered,
"Andale rapido,"
or when shadows shifted in the distance.
She was breathing hard.
Not the kind of breath that comes from walking fast
the kind that comes from carrying too much.
A child beside her.
A child inside her.
A future she was terrified might not come.
The desert sky stretched above us,
wide and watchful,
filled with stars that did nothing to show us the way.
My father and the coyote,
their faces hidden beneath baseball caps,
Adults who normally spoke loudly
now barely made a sound.
Fear had a way of quieting even the boldest voices.
I stumbled more than once,
my snow suit bunching at my knees.
My mother pulled me up each time
despite the strain on her stomach

and the exhaustion in her eyes.
She did not cry.
She did not stop.
She did not show weakness.
All she said was,
"Ven, mi amor. No te sueltes."
Come, my love. Do not let go.
Hours passed without shape or meaning.
We moved through the cold
as if walking through a dream
where time and direction dissolve.
At one point, my teddy slipped from my fingers
and fell into the sand.
I gasped and turned to reach for him,
my small hands digging until I found his arm.
My mother froze when I stopped walking,
fear flashing across her face
like a flame that burned too quickly.
When she saw I had him again,
she exhaled,
a long, trembling breath
that said more than words ever could.
We kept going.
When we finally reached safety,

my mother bent over,
hands on her knees,
breathing like someone who had escaped drowning.
As a child, I did not understand the risk.
I did not understand borders, laws, danger, or sacrifice.
All I knew was that my mother and father got us through
the night
with strength I would not fully recognize
until I became a mother myself.
Now, as an adult,
I look back at that four year old girl
in her snow suit and boots full of sand,
clutching a teddy bear against the cold,
following a woman who refused to collapse
because collapsing meant ending.
And I understand something clearly:
That night did not break me.
It formed me.
It shaped the mother I became.
It shaped the woman I am.
It taught me survival before I knew the word.
And it taught me that the body remembers
even the journeys we cannot comprehend at the time.

When I Became the Safe Space I Needed

I learned to become a safe space

not through criticism

but through awareness.

There came a moment

when both of my children felt overwhelmed,

their emotions rising together

like a changing tide.

I didn't rush to quiet the moment.

I didn't push their feelings aside.

I simply paused

and paid attention

to the current beneath the surface.

In that stillness,

I understood something important

they did not need the world managed for them.

They needed grounding.

They needed calm.

They needed someone who could stand steady

while they found their balance.

I realized my role

was not to control the waves

but to anchor the shoreline.

I am not here to reshape who they are.

I am here to hold space

for who they are becoming.

And in becoming that space for them,

I also became it for myself

a place of breath,

a place of truth,

a place where love is patient

and presence is enough.

Instructions for a Mexican Daughter

They taught me rules without speaking.
Eyes down.
Hands steady.
Heart guarded.
Dreams folded small.
But I was born with a mind
that refused confinement.
While others learned to hide,
I learned to observe.
While others played polite,
I studied the air,
the silence,
the intentions behind words.
My daughter carries that same fire.
She does not shrink.
She does not quiet herself.
She does not bow to customs
that were never written in her language.
I let her be.
Not because rebellion is required,
but because authenticity is sacred.

My Other Grandmother's Hands

My father's mother had hands that held the earth.

They were weathered,

firm,

steady,

and capable of more work

than a single lifetime should hold.

Those hands harvested,

sewed,

washed,

and prayed.

They knew the rhythm of survival

in a way that had nothing to do with weakness

and everything to do with discipline.

She was not a woman of soft edges.

Her strength came in the shape of silence,

the kind that does not break,

the kind that expects others to follow suit.

As a child,

I felt misunderstood by her.

As an adult,

I see her differently.

She was shaped by a world

that demanded endurance,

not introspection.

What she could not say,

she taught through action.

And though I walk a different path,

I carry her resilience

in the quiet places of my spirit.

Motherhood Without a Map

I became a mother
without a guide,
without a script,
without a pattern to follow.
Instead, I carried stories
of women who worked
with the patience of stone
and the strength of rivers.
I do not recreate their silence.
I honor their endurance
by choosing a gentler form of strength.
I listen.
I observe.
I adapt.
Motherhood is not a performance for me.

It is a pilgrimage,
a quiet journey inward,
where I meet the child I once was
and the woman I am still becoming.

My Mother's Shadow and My Own Light

My mother lived her life in long shadows.
Not because she lacked light,
but because she was taught to stand behind others
even when she carried the weight of entire worlds.
She knew how to endure
without asking for permission.
Her silence was a shield,
and her strength was a language
no one ever translated for her.
I watched her move through life
as if survival were a rhythm in her blood.
Every step deliberate.
Every decision precise.
Every sacrifice made without witness.
But I inherited more than her shadows.
I inherited her instincts,
her awareness,
her ability to sense truth
even when it was unspoken.
The difference is that I do not remain in her shadows.
I step beside them,
carrying both her wisdom and my own clarity.

Where she endured,
I question.
Where she held silence,
I speak carefully,
choosing words that heal
instead of words that wound.
Where she hid her weariness,
I allow rest
without shame.
I am not here to escape her legacy.
I am here to illuminate it
so my children do not inherit darkness
without understanding its source.

The Instructions My Culture Forgot to Give

They gave me many rules
but forgot to give me guidance.
They told me how to serve
but not how to receive.
How to endure
but not how to recover.
How to obey
but not how to trust myself.
They taught me to hold everything in
until the heart became a locked room.
Yet even locked rooms
have windows.
Through those windows
I learned to breathe for myself.
To think beyond tradition.
To question with dignity.
To honor my culture
without imprisoning my spirit.
I am the daughter of a lineage
that survived without instruction.
And now
I teach what they could not say.

When My Daughter Looked at Me Differently

One afternoon, my daughter looked at me with a gaze

that felt older than her years,

as if she were seeing me for the first time

not as her mother

but as a woman with her own history.

She had asked a simple question.

Something about why I prefer to be by myself

and having control of my environment.

I paused before answering.

Not because the question frightened me,

but because it required honesty

that children sense before they understand.

I told her that my mind listens

in ways other people do not notice.

That I feel more

than I can explain out loud.

That I move through the world

like someone observing many layers at once.

She nodded slowly,

absorbing my words

as if she recognized them.

Then she sat closer to me,

her small shoulder resting against mine,

and whispered,

"I feel that too."

In that moment,

our connection shifted.

Not away from mother and child,

but deeper into recognition.

She saw me not as someone who demands understanding

but as someone who offers it.

And in her whisper,

I heard the future learning to speak.

The Thread That Did Not Break

From grandmother
to mother
to daughter,
a single thread runs through us.
Not the thread of suffering,
but the thread of endurance.
A line of women
who held the world
without letting it crush them.
This thread is not frayed.
It is woven from memory,
intuition,
and an ancient strength
that does not ask for praise.
I do not cut this thread.
I guide it,
shape it,
and pass it forward
without the knots
that once bound me.

Becoming the First Woman in

My Line to Rest

One day, I realized I was doing

something no woman in my family had done before me.

I stopped moving.

I allowed myself to rest.

Not because I was weak,

but because I finally understood

that rest is not surrender.

Rest is permission.

My grandmothers could not rest.

Life demanded too much from them.

My mother paused only when exhaustion

forced her to stop.

But I rest with intention.

I rest to create space for clarity.

I rest to listen to the whispers inside me

that were buried under years of urgency.

In my rest,

I found wisdom.

And that wisdom

is what I pass to my children,

so they grow into adults

who do not equate stillness

with failure.

I am the first woman in my lineage

to rest without apology.

And because of that,

I will not be the last.

Chapter 3: The Girl Who Mirrors My Sky

When I Saw Myself in Her Eyes

She looked at me one morning with eyes that held a quiet knowing.
Not fear.
Not confusion.
Recognition.

As if she discovered a hidden passage between her world and mine.

Her gaze said what words could not:
We were shaped from the same silence,
cut from the same thread
of awareness.

She is not my reflection.
She is my continuation.

The Day She Heard What Others Missed

We stood in a grocery store when she tugged my sleeve.
The room seemed calm to most people,
but her expression sharpened
as if the air itself had changed.

She whispered, "Mom, do you hear that?"

At first I didn't.
Then I sensed it
a faint metallic vibration from a freezer in the back.
Barely audible.
But sharp enough to sting.

She pressed her hands to her ears.
I placed mine on her shoulder.

"I hear it now," I said.

Her body softened.
Not because the sound stopped,
but because she wasn't alone in noticing it.

Her sensitivity is not fragility.
It is early wisdom.

Lines of Light

She walks through the world
following paths no one else sees.

Her instincts are old.
Her silence is deliberate.
Her presence is whole.

She is young,
yet guided by a compass
that never points wrong.

The Moment She Realized I Understand Her

One evening she sat curled on the floor,

breathing fast,

thoughts tangled.

I sat beside her quietly

until her breath matched mine.

She looked up and whispered,

"You feel like this too sometimes."

I nodded.

Recognition was enough.

She leaned into me

and the storm within her softened.

Seed of Strength

I planted no expectations in her

only space.

Only presence.

Only truth.

From that,

she grows in directions

I never had permission to explore.

She is not shaped.

She is unfolding.

Her Sensitivity Is Her Superpower

She notices shifts others never sense.

A tremor in someone's voice.

A silence stretched too thin.

A room holding unspoken tension.

People misunderstand her awareness as fragility.

But it is intuition.

It is insight.

It is wisdom in motion.

My role is not to harden her

but to protect the softness that makes her wise.

The Way She Studies the World

She pauses often,

not out of hesitation

but intention.

She listens to the air,

to warmth,

to subtle changes.

When she closes her eyes

and moves to a rhythm only she feels,

I recognize the freedom

I worked years to reclaim.

The Language Between Us

We speak without speaking.

Her eyes ask questions

her mouth has not shaped.

My silence answers

in a way words never could.

Delicate.

Precise.

Sacred.

When She Reminds Me of the Girl I Was

Sometimes she hums softly,

or tilts her head to the light,

and I see the child I once was

the version before the world insisted

I become "less."

She steps aside when she needs space

with ease I never had.

She is not my reflection.

She is my reminder.

She Is Not Afraid of Her Voice

She speaks when she has something to say.

She is quiet when silence is honesty.

Her words are steady,

rooted,

intentional.

Her voice is not loud

because it doesn't need to be.

Daughter of Insight

She is the quiet dawn after a long night,
soft enough to calm,
bright enough to reveal.

She reads truth without effort
and honors silence without fear.

She is not my shadow.
She is not my mirror.

She is the rising light
of a story that finally feels seen.

The Quiet Thread Between Us

She has always moved toward me
not with urgency,
but with certainty.
From the moment she could walk,
she walked toward my voice.
From the moment she could speak,
she whispered my name in the dark
as if confirming I was still the anchor
she felt in her bones.
Our bond did not grow in dramatic moments.
It grew in the soft spaces,
in the hours unnoticed by the world.
I remember one afternoon clearly.
The house was warm with late sunlight,
draping the walls in muted gold.
She sat cross-legged on the carpet,
drawing shapes only she understood.
I watched her in silence,
careful not to disturb the little universe
she was creating with her hands.
Then she looked up

not abruptly,
but slowly,
as if she sensed my gaze
before her eyes found mine.
She smiled,
a small, knowing curve of the mouth
that held more understanding
than many adults manage to convey.
She didn't speak.
She didn't need to.
She scooted closer,
inch by inch,
until her shoulder pressed against mine.
Her breathing matched my breathing.
Her small hand rested on my knee
as though claiming her place
without asking permission.
There was no tension.
No need for explanation.
Just presence.
Quiet.
Whole.
She has a way of settling beside me
that feels like a conversation
beneath all sound.

Sometimes she curls herself into my side
while we watch the ceiling fan spin,
her head resting on my shoulder
as if we are both listening
for a message carried in the air.
She notices when my energy shifts.
She studies the silence around me.
If my mind grows heavy,
she leans her weight against me gently,
her warmth reminding me
that I am not alone
in my intensity.
She mirrors only the parts of me
that matter
the calm,
the intuition,
the observation,
the quiet knowing
that we feel things before we look at them.
Our bond is not dramatic
or loud
or filled with grand gestures.
It is made of small touches,
shared stillness,
the exchanges of glances
that say more than words can manage.

She is the girl
who senses my storms
before the clouds arrive.
And I am the mother
who gives her space
to remain exactly
as she was always meant to be.
We are connected
not by expectation
but by recognition.
She is not just my daughter.
She is the quiet thread
that pulls me gently
back into myself.

When She Walks Into the Room

When she walks into the room

the air remembers how to soften.

Even the dust motes seem to pause,

hovering lightly

as if listening for her breath.

She carries silence like a lantern,

not to hide within it

but to illuminate the corners

other people never see.

Her footsteps fall

with the gentleness of petals

and the certainty of roots.

She is young,

yet her presence feels seasoned

as though her spirit

has walked long roads

before arriving here.

When she speaks,

her voice is a quiet flute,

lifting thoughts like wings

to the rafters of my mind.

When she is still,

I learn from her

how to inhabit the moment

without crowding it,

how to breathe

without expectation,

how to feel

without unraveling.

She does not command attention;

she invites it.

She does not demand understanding;

she evokes it.

And I, who spent years

trying to become smaller, quieter,

learn from her daily

that gentleness is not the opposite of strength

it is its truest form.

The Daughter Who Teaches Me Light

She gathers sunlight

the way others gather stones

carefully,

deliberately,

as if warmth itself

were a treasure to be saved.

I watch her lift her face

toward an open window

and close her eyes,

letting the brightness fold itself

into every quiet place inside her.

She teaches me

that the world is gentler

than I remember.

She teaches me

that softness is not weakness

but a choice,

a tender defiance

against harshness.
When she laughs,
the sound rises lightly,
as though the sky
were pulling it upward
to keep for later.
When she cries,
her tears are honest,
not hidden,
never shameful.
She has not learned
to fear her own vulnerability,
and I protect that fiercely.
She teaches me
that strength does not need armor,
that courage arrives quietly,
that healing begins
where truth is allowed to breathe.
And in her presence
I remember the girl I was
before the world taught me

to swallow my light.

She is my daughter

but sometimes

I wonder if she is also

my teacher,

my reminder,

my gentle compass

guiding me back

to the parts of myself

I thought I lost.

Chapter 4: The Boy Made of Constellations

The First Time I Held a Universe

He arrived with a presence that shifted the room.

Dimples like hidden doorways.

Curls spiraling like unanswered questions.

He observed instead of cried.

He studied instead of reacted.

Holding him felt like holding a star

just beginning to form.

The Boy Who Speaks in Echoes of Dawn

His words rise like mist from still water.

Soft outlines first,

then gentle shape.

When language hesitates,

his eyes speak

dark, aware,

filled with meaning unspoken.

He communicates deeply,

just not in the world's expected format.

He Carries Fire and Softness Together

There is a glow beneath his quiet,

a heat that does not demand attention

yet radiates.

His laughter is sudden warmth.

His tenderness arrives without warning

a head against my arm,

a shoulder leaning into mine.

Intensity and gentleness

rest easily within him.

When He Looks Into My Eyes

He studies me with slow intention,

as though reading a map carved into my features.

He lifts his hand to my cheek,

grounding himself,

and anchoring me too.

In that stillness,

connection replaces speech.

Storm and Sanctuary

His energy shifts like a sky turning.

Breath quickens.

Hands move with urgency.

And then

he comes to me quietly,

leans into my shoulder,

and the room settles.

His storms teach rhythm,

not fear.

His Strength Does Not Announce Itself

He faces a loud world

with steady determination.

His resilience is subtle,

but undeniable.

He is not defined by difficulty.

He is defined by endurance.

The Weightless Moments

Sometimes he moves through rooms

with almost no sound,

as if gravity treats him gently.

He pauses in doorways,

listening to things others ignore.

He stands between worlds

the visible

and the one only he navigates.

The Touch That Speaks More Than Words

When words retreat,

he reaches for my hand.

Not grasping

inviting.

His touch carries

certainty, trust,

and understanding

that language often fails.

The Mirror That Shows Me Truth

His glance reveals what I hide.

He notices tension

before I speak it.

He senses heaviness

even when I smile.

Through him,

I see what I would otherwise avoid.

The World He Builds Inside Himself

Inside him exists a landscape

arranged by intuition,

not instruction.

He allows me near it

through gestures,

through shared glances,

through rare smiles

that open like small doors.

The Boy Who Walks Between Stars

He is made of quiet fire,

steady glow,

and unspoken brilliance.

He does not walk behind me

or ahead of me.

He walks beside me

a constellation

learning its own name.

Moonbinder

He watches the moon

as if it whispers to him

in a forgotten language.

Its pale glow settles over him,

calming what the world agitates.

He lifts his chin toward it

not reaching,

recognizing.

The moon does not ask him to speak.

It simply shines.

And he understands that.

The Night He Reached for the Sky

We stood outside in cool darkness.

He paused mid-step,

hand rising toward the moon

in a gesture of greeting,

not longing.

His breath slowed.

His eyes softened.

His entire being aligned

with that distant light.

He isn't admiring it.

He is connecting to it

echo to echo.

Moon Language

The moon speaks to him

the way the world does not.

Under its glow,

his mind settles,

his body eases,

his thoughts align.

He is not looking at the moon

for beauty.

He is studying its stillness

its calm,

its certainty,

its silent power.

He understands it instinctively.

Perhaps because in its presence

he sees himself.

He Walks the Edge of Hidden Worlds

He knows the quiet places

where light barely reaches,

where sound folds inward

and breath becomes the only steady thing.

He walks those spaces

without fear,

with an instinct that feels ancient

as though he has traveled them

long before he belonged to me.

Sometimes he stops

and tilts his head,

listening to something

the rest of us were never built to hear.

Not danger.

Not ghosts.

But the subtle shift

in the atmosphere

that warns his body

before his mind can explain.

And when that shift comes

when the walls feel closer

and the world tightens around him

I watch him reach inward,

searching for the thread

that leads him back.

It is never a straight line.

It never follows logic.

But it always leads him home.

And when he finds it,

when the tension leaves his shoulders

and his gaze softens again,

he turns toward me

with a look that breaks me open.

A look that says

I made it through.

I am here.

You stayed.

He knows the quiet places

in ways I never will.

And yet,

he lets me walk beside him,

even when the path is dim,

even when the terrain shifts,

even when the world inside him

trembles like thin glass.

He does not need me

to pull him from the dark.

He only needs me

to not disappear

when the shadow falls.

And so I stay,

steady,

present,

unmoving,

until he steps forward

into the light

that is uniquely his.

When His Hands Tremble,

I Become the Earth Beneath Him

His hands tremble sometimes

when the world widens too quickly,

when sounds stack

and lights flicker

and movement becomes

a labyrinth he cannot navigate.

He does not cry out.

He does not call for me.

He simply looks,

a glance filled with raw truth,

a plea wrapped in instinct,

a request that needs no words.

And I go to him.

Not rushing,

not overwhelming,

but slowly,

like approaching a startled bird

that needs gentleness

more than anything.

I kneel beside him,

my presence a whisper,

my breath steady and low,

offering calm

instead of correction.

He grips my arm

with quiet desperation,

the pressure steady,

not painful,

just grounding.

His fingers clench,

release,

clench again,

trying to find a rhythm

inside the chaos.

I let him hold on

until the tremor softens,

until his shoulders lower,

until his breath returns

to its natural cadence.

In those moments,

I am not simply his mother.

I am his anchor.

His boundary.

His shelter.

His certainty.

And when he finally lifts his head

and meets my eyes,

there is something sacred

in that small victory.

Because he knows

that no matter how dark

his inner world becomes,

he can return to me,

and I will be

the ground he stands on.

The Boy Who Borrowed the Song

There are days
when he seems to belong
more to the music
than to the moment.
His ears tilt gently,
as if catching a melody
threaded through the air
a sound only he can hear,
a language he understands
better than words.
He reaches toward the rhythm,
fingers tapping,
body swaying,
as though syncing himself
to an unseen conductor
who guides him back to calm.
On those days,
he is quiet
not withdrawn,
not overwhelmed,

just tuned
to a frequency
that keeps him safe.
I watch him,
and I see a child
who carries symphonies
in the chambers of his mind.
Not chaos.
Not misbehavior.
But a harmony so intricate
that the world mistakes it
for distance.
Even when his feet
stand steady where he is,
his mind drifts
into a place
where sound becomes shelter
a place of rhythm
I will never fully enter.
But then
he looks at me.
The music softens.
The world settles.
The beat steadies
into something we share.
He walks toward me

with the slow, sure steps
of a child who trusts
the sound of his own heartbeat
only when he feels mine.
He leans into my chest,
and I feel the weight of him
solid, warm,
unquestionably here.
He does not belong entirely
to silence or to sound.
He belongs
to the space between,
where melodies protect him,
where noise cannot reach him,
where love
does not need volume
to be heard.
And every time he returns to me,
I am reminded
that even the loudest worlds
quiet themselves
for the children
who find peace
in a single song.

The Shadow He Takes My Hand Through

There are moments
when his world tilts
without warning.
A shift behind his eyes,
a tension in his jaw,
a stillness that is not calm
but preparation.
It begins quietly,
a tightening in his posture
as if bracing for impact
from something no one else can see.
His breath shortens.
His fingers curl inward.
His gaze drops to the floor
as though the ground itself
might steady him.
The room does not change—
but *he* does.
Subtle at first,
then unmistakable.

I recognize the signs instantly.
Not because I studied them
in books or training manuals,
but because they are etched into me
the way stars imprint themselves
on the night sky.
I move to him slowly,
never forcing myself into his space.
I kneel nearby,
close enough to reach him
but far enough
to let him choose.
His hand hesitates in the air,
hovering between reaching out
and retreating.
Then, with a soft exhale,
he extends it
not fully,
not confidently,
but enough for me to take it
without fear of overwhelming him.
His fingers wrap around mine,
shaky at first,
then firm

as the tremor inside him
searches for something solid.
In that moment,
I am not holding a child's hand.
I am holding a bridge
the fragile connection
between his internal storm
and the world outside it.
The shadow he moves through
is not darkness.
It is distortion.
A place where sound bends,
where light thickens,
where sensations collide
like waves in a storm.
But he does not walk through it alone.
He guides me,
step by step,
through the terrain of his mind
as though letting me witness
the landscape others cannot understand.
He presses his forehead to my shoulder,
and the room shifts
not back to normal,

but back to something bearable.
His breath evens.
The tension leaves his hands.
His body softens
in a way that lets me know
the worst has passed.
We do not speak.
Speech is unnecessary
in this sacred exchange.
He simply leans,
and I simply hold,
and in the quiet of that moment,
hope unfolds
like a small flower
in a place where flowers rarely grow.
He lifts his head
and meets my eyes
the storm behind him,
the calm ahead.
And I realize again
what I learn every time:
He does not need rescue.
He needs presence.
He needs someone

who will not abandon him
when the shadow rises.
Someone who will walk with him
through every distortion,
every tremor,
every unfamiliar path
his mind takes him through.
I am that someone
not because I am strong,
but because he trusts me enough
to take my hand
when his world shifts.
And that trust
is the purest form of love
I have ever known.

Chapter 5: The Inner Landscape

The Architecture of My Mind

My mind has always felt like a structure built with hidden rooms.

Some rooms are bright, filled with ideas that arrive all at once.

Others are dim, steady, quiet places where thoughts gather slowly.

I have learned which rooms to approach with patience, and which ones to protect from the world outside.

This inner architecture is not chaotic.

It is intricate.

It is mine.

When the World Feels Too Loud

There are days when voices feel layered,

when lights sharpen instead of shine,

when movement vibrates through my body

like static I cannot switch off.

People ask why I step away,

why I pause mid-sentence,

why I close my eyes.

It is not weakness.

It is preservation.

I step back before the overwhelm

swallows my ability to think clearly.

The Mask I Learned to Wear

There is a version of me the world finds easy to understand.

Calm expression.

Quiet posture.

Measured tone.

None of it is dishonest.

It is simply the version the world accepts

without asking too many questions.

Masking is not pretending.

It is protection.

A way of navigating spaces

that demand simplicity

from minds built with depth.

I am learning when to wear the mask

and when to take it off.

When Silence Becomes Language

Silence is not emptiness.

Silence is where my thoughts finally settle.

In silence,

I can hear the shape of my own emotions

before they turn into words.

I rebuild myself in quiet.

I return to clarity in quiet.

Silence is not something I fear.

It is a place that welcomes me back

whenever the world becomes overwhelming.

The Sensory Thread

There is a thread inside me
that reacts to every shift in the world.
A faint hum can unravel my focus.
A sudden brightness can knock me off center.
A crowded room can feel like falling
without moving at all.
And still
A soft breeze can ground me.
A familiar texture can calm me instantly.
A steady voice can guide me back
with just a few words.
This thread is not broken.
It is simply tuned differently.

The Truth I No Longer Hide

I used to believe I needed to justify myself
just to belong.
Why I needed quiet.
Why I stepped away.
Why my emotions were vivid.
Why my mind worked differently.
I do not explain myself anymore.
I exist as I am,
with depth,
with sensitivity,
with intention.
And now,
I no longer shrink
to make others comfortable.
I no longer apologize
for thinking quickly,
working hard,
or dreaming beyond the limits
they set for themselves.
I no longer carry guilt
for being an overachiever,
for wanting more,

for doing more,
for accomplishing what others said
was impossible.
I used to dim my light
so no one felt overshadowed.
I softened my voice,
held back my ideas,
pretended I didn't know the answer,
just to avoid being labeled
"too much"
or "a know-it-all."
But the truth is,
my confidence
was never the problem.
Their insecurity
was never my responsibility.
I am not too much.
I am not unfinished.
I am not a threat
to anyone who truly knows themselves.
I am simply built
in another direction
and I no longer hide
the brilliance of that path.

How I Learned to Stay

There was a time

I lived outside myself

smoothing edges,

quieting thoughts,

shrinking needs.

Trying to make my internal world

fit into a shape I did not choose.

But one day,

while sitting alone in stillness,

I felt a pull inward

soft, certain, undeniable.

An invitation to return

to my true form.

And I accepted it.

Not because it was easy,

but because authenticity

is the only place

where breathing feels natural.

The Day I Owned My Name

There is power

in saying autistic

without lowering my voice.

Power in naming myself

without apology.

Not as something broken.

Not as something lacking.

But as something true.

My identity is not a burden.

It is clarity.

It is alignment.

It is understanding myself

on my own terms.

Becoming the Change

When I see my daughter
absorbing light with her whole being,
or my son
finding stillness beneath the night sky,
I recognize pieces of myself in them.
Not the struggle
the strength.
The intuition.
The depth.
The sensitivity.
I protect them
the way I once needed someone
to protect me.
I give them room
instead of restriction and criticism.
Support
instead of silence.
Understanding
instead of pressure.
I break nothing in them.
I only break the cycle
that once narrowed me.

The Center of the Constellation

I used to believe

I was the weak link in my family's chain.

But now I see

I am the center of the constellation

the one who understands the languages

of both light and shadow.

My daughter mirrors my gentleness.

My son mirrors my depth.

I stand between them,

not as a barrier

but as a guide

who finally understands

her own design.

The Hour the Air Turns Heavy

There is an hour

when the air turns heavy

without warning.

Not night.

Not morning.

An hour outside of time.

It settles in my bones first

a weight that pulls downward

in slow, deliberate increments.

Anxiety gathers quietly,

sinking into the corners of my thoughts

like water collecting beneath a floorboard.

My pulse stumbles.

My chest tightens.

My hands tremble

as the body braces

for something unseen.

Then panic rises

swift, cold,

disconnecting everything at once.

The room tilts.

Logic thins.

My sense of self wavers

as if standing behind glass

that no one else can see.

When the episode fades,

depression slips into the space

panic leaves behind.

Not loud.

Not dramatic.

Just a slow dimming

an erosion of color and interest

until even movement

feels like wading through thick water.

These states are not weakness.

They are battles

fought in stillness,

without witnesses,

without applause.

And yet,

I do not break.

I breathe through it.

I stay through it.

I wait until the world settles

back into place.

Every time the air turns heavy,

I rise again,

lifting it bit by bit

until the weight becomes mine to carry

instead of something that consumes me.

The House With the Locked Staircase

There is a house I enter only when the world becomes too
sharp.
It is not a real house.
It has no address.
But it lives inside me
with hallways I know by memory
and corridors I avoid until absolutely necessary.
I do not walk into it.
I *fall* into it
without warning,
without explanation,
as though the floor beneath my life
suddenly opens.
The door closes behind me
with a sound I can never fully recall,
only feel:
a heavy thud
that tells me I will not leave quickly.

The house is dim.

Not dark—

dim,

with corners that blur

and shadows that seem to shift

even when I stand completely still.

Anxiety lives in the first room.

Not as a creature

but as a presence.

A faint humming in the walls,

a tremor in the floorboards,

a vibration that crawls up my spine

and settles behind my eyes.

The room looks harmless:

bare walls,

dust floating in narrow strips of light.

But the air moves strangely,

too fast,

too thin,

as if it refuses to stay long enough

for me to breathe it.

My chest tightens here.

My thoughts race,

chasing each other in circles

until none of them make sense.

There is a staircase leading upward,

but no matter how many times I try to climb it,

the steps shift beneath my feet

longer,

shorter,

disappearing entirely.

Panic waits at the top of the stairs,

and it knows I cannot reach it.

It watches,

silent and cold,

a figure made of stillness

and distance.

When panic comes,

it does not scream.

It stares.

It stares so intensely

that I forget how to swallow,

how to speak,

how to exist without shaking.

The room bends,

the air wavers,

and the floor seems to tilt

though I know it does not actually move.

I grip the banister

that isn't fully solid

and tell myself to breathe

even when breath feels foreign.

Eventually

always eventually

panic withdraws,

not defeated,

but bored with me.

It retreats up the staircase

I never reached,

melting into the shadows

like a ghost slipping behind a closed door.

When panic leaves,

depression enters.

Not from above.

From below.

It rises through the floor,

seeping through the boards

like dark water,

slow and steady,

surrounding my feet first,

cooling my ankles,

pulling gently,

not forcefully.

Depression does not push me down.

It invites me to sink.

It opens a second door

to a room without edges

a room where everything is muted,

not silent,

just softened into a colorless blur.

The walls are neither near nor far.

The floor is neither firm nor soft.

Time stretches thin,

like a thread pulled tight

but never breaking.

In that room,

my body feels too heavy to move

and too restless to stay still.

My thoughts dim

as though someone turned down the brightness

on the inside of my skull.

But here is the secret I learned,

and the reason I survive this place:

In the very center of the room,

beneath the quiet and the weight,

there is a small light.

It is not warm.

It is not bright.

But it is steady.

A flame that refuses to go out

no matter how thick the gloom becomes.

When I focus on it,

the room shifts.

Barely.

But enough.

The walls regain shape.

The air warms slightly.

The floor grows solid beneath my feet.

And slowly,

slowly,

I stand.

The door behind me unlocks

with a soft click

the first sound I have heard in hours

that doesn't feel threatening.

I walk back through the hallway

into the room where anxiety hums,

but the vibration does not climb into my thoughts this time.

I pass the staircase

without trying to climb it.

Panic is gone now,

and the steps remain silent.

I reach the entryway.

The door opens.

The world outside feels too bright at first,

too loud,

too close

but it is real,

and I walk into it.

The house remains behind me,

but I no longer fear it.

I know its halls.

I know its rooms.

I know where the light waits

and how to find it

when the air turns heavy again.

I survived it once.

I will survive it every time.

Chapter 6: The Woman Who Did Not Break

The Rooms I Built Myself

There was a time when I believed strength was something loud.
Something performed.
Something proven with force.
But strength, for me, came quietly.
Not in triumph or shouting,
but in the decision to continue
again and again
even when the world misunderstood my inner rhythm.
I learned early that I processed life differently.
That I felt everything on frequencies other people could not hear.
That sound hit me deeper,
that emotions ran sharper,
that thoughts came layered like pages of a book
flipped all at once.
People called it too much.
Too sensitive.
Too intense.

Too emotional.

They were wrong.

This intensity was not a flaw.

It was a compass.

It guided me through rooms

where others wandered without direction.

I became a woman who saw beneath the surface.

Who sensed tension before it was spoken.

Who read truth in silence.

Who felt storms coming before the clouds formed.

Not a victim of sensitivity,

but a master of perception.

As I grew,

I realized the world prefers people

who dilute themselves.

People who quiet their instincts.

People who shrink their depth.

People who follow the script

instead of rewriting it.

I did not shrink.

I adjusted.

I adapted.

I observed.

Not to erase myself,

but to survive long enough

to understand my own mind.
And once I understood it,
everything shifted.
I stopped apologizing for needing space
when the noise grew sharp.
I stopped masking to make others comfortable.
I stopped carrying guilt
for being wired differently.
I stopped explaining my existence
as though it required permission.
I stepped into my truth,
unshaken by anyone else's discomfort.
And slowly,
I built myself from the inside out
not from what the world demanded,
but from what I needed:
Clarity.
Depth.
Peace.
Fire.
Faith in my own resilience.
I became the woman
who did not break.
Not because life was gentle with me,

but because my spirit refused to shatter.
Because my mind, wired in its own direction,
created structures strong enough
to withstand every storm.
And now
I stand fully formed,
fully aware,
fully myself.
I am not defined by struggle.
I am defined by survival
with my essence intact.
I am not tragic.
I am not fragile.
I am not incomplete.
I am the result
of everything I endured
and everything I chose
not to surrender.
I am whole
because I built myself that way.

The Weight I Learned to Carry Without Breaking

I learned to lift

the heaviness inside me

without letting it crush me.

The weight was never mine alone

it came from expectation,

from misunderstanding,

from the world demanding simplicity,

from a mind made of constellations.

I carried that weight

not in silence,

but with intention.

I set it down

when my hands trembled.

I picked it up

when my spirit steadied.

I learned its shape,

its edges,

its shifting center.

And slowly,

I became stronger

than everything that once threatened

to pull me under.

The weight did not disappear.

I simply grew strong enough

to hold it

without losing myself.

The Spine Made of Fire

My strength is not soft.
It is not quiet.
It is not gentle light.
It is fire
the kind that does not burn the world,
but forges the person carrying it.
I have walked through seasons
designed to break people
who did not know their own power.
But I knew mine.
It lived in the way I stood tall
even when the ground trembled.
It lived in the way I kept moving
when every instinct said freeze.
It lived in the way I kept loving
even when the world felt cold.
My spine is not made of bone.
It is made of fire
and I rise
because there is something ancient in me
that refuses to fall.

The Day I Chose Myself

There was no audience.

No applause.

No dramatic revelation.

Just a quiet decision

in a quiet room

on an ordinary day.

I looked at the version of myself

the world preferred—

the agreeable one,

the masked one,

the diluted one—

and I let her go.

Not with anger.

Not with grief.

Just release.

I stepped into myself fully—

into truth,

into clarity,

into the shape I was always meant to be.

I chose myself

without hesitation,

without guilt,

without explanation.

And in choosing myself,

I became someone

I no longer had to hide from.

The Man Who Matched My Silence

I never imagined someone would understand the quiet
places in me
without demanding I fill them with sound.
For so long, I believed partnership meant performance.
Smiling at the right moments,
laughing on cue,
translating my inner world
into something digestible
for someone who could never truly see me.
But when he came into my life,
he did not ask for a performance.
He watched.
He listened.
He noticed the pauses between my sentences,
the way I pulled back from noise,
the way my emotions deepened
instead of widening.
Most people are startled
by intensity wrapped in calm.
He was not.

He recognized it,
not because he studied it,
but because he lived something similar.
He didn't flinch
when I struggled to speak my feelings.
He didn't rush me
when I needed time to decompress.
He didn't question
why my mind shifted between worlds
the way weather changes direction.
He simply stayed.
A presence beside me,
not pushing,
not pulling,
not demanding.
He spoke the kind of language
that does not come from words
but from understanding.
A shared wavelength
beneath the obvious.
It was strange at first,
to be seen without being deciphered.
To be loved without being decoded.
To be accepted

without being rearranged.
He was not perfect,
and neither was I.
But our imperfections aligned
like the pattern of two broken mirrors
reflecting a clearer whole.
We learned each other's rhythms.
We built trust on quiet nights
and unspoken thoughts.
We found companionship
not in our sameness,
but in our matching strangeness.
I realized then:
I had not been searching for someone normal.
I had been searching for someone real,
someone whose oddness
resonated with mine
in a way that felt like coming home.
And I found him.

When Two Unusual Souls Choose Each Other

We did not fall in love quickly.

We unfolded slowly

layer by layer,

moment by moment,

as though time itself knew

we needed gentleness.

He once told me

there was something familiar about me,

a recognition he could not place.

I felt it too

a strange sense

that our minds curved in similar directions,

that our thoughts bent around the world

in patterns that mirrored each other.

Our connection did not spark like lightning.

It glowed like embers

steady, slow-burning,

almost imperceptible until suddenly

it warmed everything.

We understood each other's overwhelm.

We respected each other's space.

We navigated silence

with the ease of two people

who preferred presence

over noise.

When I needed to shut down,

he did not take it personally.

He simply dimmed the lights

and sat near me,

breathing softly,

letting me return at my own pace.

When he felt the heaviness of his own mind,

I sat beside him

with the same quiet loyalty.

We were not rescuing each other.

We were witnessing.

Honoring.

Holding space

without expectation.

The world had always told me

I was too much—

too deep,

too intense,

too sensitive,

too quiet.

But with him,

I was exactly enough.

And he was enough for me.

We did not complete each other.

We complemented each other.

Two unusual souls

choosing,

day after day,

to stay intertwined

because the world made more sense

when we walked it together.

When Two Shadows Found the Same Light

We were both shadows

wandering different corners of the world,

searching for warmth

we had learned to expect

only from ourselves.

Then one day,

our shadows crossed.

Not dramatically,

not like a storybook,

but quietly

a merging of edges

that felt accidental

and inevitable at once.

He did not brighten my darkness.

He illuminated his own

beside mine.

Two muted shapes

walking toward a shared horizon,

learning each other's silhouettes

in the soft half-light.

We found solace

not in perfection

but in recognition.

Not in saving

but in staying.

Not in filling each other

but in remaining whole

side by side.

We were shadows once,

separate and wandering

now we stand together,

forming a shape the world cannot name

but we know is ours.

The Gravity Between Us

He has a gravity

I cannot explain.

Not a pull

that drags or demands

a pull

that steadies.

A force

that reminds me

I am allowed to exist

without shrinking.

When my thoughts scatter

like feathers in wind,

he gathers the pieces

without insisting they form a shape

before they are ready.

When his mind folds inward,

I sit beside him

with the calm that says

take your time,

I am not going anywhere.

Our gravity is not romance.

It is resonance.

A frequency we share

because our minds

speak in patterns others don't hear.

He does not fix me.

I do not fix him.

We simply align

two planets

with orbits that finally

make sense.

The Strange Belongs to Us

He once laughed

and told me

we were the strangest pair he knew.

Not because we were odd to others

but because our minds

fit together

like mismatched puzzle pieces

that made a new picture

once combined.

We think differently.

Speak differently.

Feel differently.

And instead of hiding that,

we treat it like treasure.

He calls my intensity

a gift.

I call his quiet

a strength.

He sees my spiraling thoughts

not as problems

but as galaxies.

I see his stillness

not as distance

but as depth.

We are strange,

yes

but the strange belongs to us.

And in a world that demands conformity,

choosing each other

is the most beautiful rebellion we have.

Chapter 7: The Mind That Learns, Remembers, and Rises

The Mind That Refuses to Sleep

My mind has always held its own rhythm.
While the world powers down at night,
mine hums with possibility.
Ideas arrive fully formed.
Memories resurface for sorting.
Instinct becomes louder than logic.
And silence becomes the only place
my thoughts can breathe freely.
It is not restlessness.
It is processing.
It is clarity.
It is survival shaped into focus.
I walk softly through dim hallways,
a shadow moving in familiar spaces,
not lost,
but recalibrating.
This is when I understand myself best,
in the hours when the world sleeps
and my mind finally has the space
to stretch.

The Invisible Thread of Intuition

There is a knowing in me
that does not come from facts
or explanations
or long conversations.
It comes from energy.
Subtle shifts.
Faint signals.
Unspoken truths.
As a child, adults told me I was dramatic.
As an adult, I know better.
What others miss,
I sense long before it is spoken.
This intuition has saved me,
guided me,
and illuminated rooms
before they turned dark.
It is not fear.
It is perception.
It is the gift beneath my sensitivity.
I follow that invisible thread
the way others follow maps,
with trust,
with certainty,
with reverence
for the wisdom carved into my nervous system.

The Comfort I Built With My Own Hands

There is one object
that has remained constant
through every version of my life:
my bear.
Soft.
Worn.
Reliable.
It has absorbed tears
I never spoke aloud
and held the weight
of emotions I could not explain.
This is not childish.
This is grounding.
This is survival.
This is continuity.
While others numb with substances,
I learned to self-soothe
with fabric and familiarity.
My bear is not a relic of childhood,
it is a reminder
that the child inside me
always knew exactly what she needed.

When Grief Arrived Too Early

I was eleven

when grief took shape in my life.

My grandfather,

my father's father,

was the man I understood as a father figure

when my own father was still learning

how to be someone I could reach.

I mourned him

before I understood healing.

I mourned him

with a depth that surprised even me.

He was steady.

Quiet.

Present.

A man who cared deeply

without needing to say the words.

Losing him felt like losing a piece of safety.

Not the kind built from words,

but the kind built from presence.

As I grew older,

I began to understand my father differently.

Not as someone who failed me,

but as someone who was still becoming.

He did not drink.

He did not disappear.

He did not choose destruction.

He chose family,

even if connection

was a language he had to learn slowly.

I see his effort now.

I appreciate the man he was

and the man he is still trying to be.

Grief softened that understanding,

turning what once felt like absence

into a quiet form of respect.

The Brother I Protected

My brother and I
have a bond difficult to explain
to anyone outside our family.
Five years apart,
yet I often felt older than the space suggests
not by age,
but by responsibility.
I watched over him.
Protected him.
Translated the world for him
in ways I did not yet know
I was translating for myself as well.
There are things about his inner world
I do not name publicly,
because they belong to him
and not to my narrative.
But I can say this:
I understood him
before I understood myself.
And protecting him
taught me how to protect my own children later
with patience,
with instinct,
with a loyalty
that does not bend.

The Art of Pretending I Understood

Social Rules

For most of my life,

I observed people

the way others study novels,

analyzing patterns,

dialogue,

tone shifts,

hidden motives

and unexplained tension.

Small talk made no sense to me.

Cliques were confusing.

Unspoken rules

felt like riddles written in a language

I was never given the dictionary for.

So I adapted.

I used humor as armor.

I joked when I was anxious.

I laughed too hard
when I felt out of place.
I acted confident
when I was decoding the room
in real time.
No one taught me social navigation,
I reverse-engineered it
from observation,
instinct,
and trial.
And still,
I remained myself.
Even when I didn't fully fit,
I showed up
with authenticity
and my own kind of grace.

The Woman I Am in My Work

Professionally,
I carved my path from courage,
not credentials.
I became:
a writer,
a presenter,
an advocate,
a voice that people seek
when they want someone
who understands depth
and refuses to sugarcoat reality.
It has not been simple,
but it has been meaningful.
The obstacles taught me persistence.
The misunderstandings taught me clarity.
The setbacks taught me patience.
My children taught me purpose.
Every lesson
built the woman I am today,
a woman who speaks for those
who were once silenced
by confusion, labels,
or lack of support.

The Night the House Would Not Sleep

There are nights when the house feels awake with me.

Not because anyone is moving,

but because the air itself seems to listen.

Everyone else slept.

I did not.

The hallway was soft-lit,

the refrigerator hummed,

the clock tapped out the seconds

with delicate insistence.

I held my bear in my hands,

feeling the familiar texture

steady my breath

in ways nothing else can.

I sat in the living room,

lights off,

mind bright.

Thoughts came like visitors,

families I support,

children who remind me of mine,

questions that needed gentle answers.

I didn't resist the noise inside me.

I sorted it.

Held it.

Worked through it

until it finally settled.

By dawn,

I felt lighter,

not because I slept,

but because I understood myself again.

The Last Afternoon with My Grandfather

I remember the light that day,
gold and soft,
like the world was holding its breath.
He sat in his chair by the window,
hands resting steady,
eyes half-focused on the street outside.
I sat beside him,
leaning just enough
to feel his shoulder against mine.
We didn't speak.
We didn't need to.
His presence was its own language,
a reassurance
I didn't know I would need
for the rest of my life.
When he died,
grief arrived like a fog.
But even in that fog,
I felt his hand on my shoulder,
steady,
guiding me toward the person
I would one day become.

The Day my Father Tried in His Own Way

We sat at the table
long after everyone else left.
My father shifted papers,
checked his phone,
asked awkward questions
that didn't land quite right.
Then he said,
"I saw what you do.
You help a lot of people."
Simple words.
Unpolished.
But genuine.
I didn't dismiss it.
I let it stand.
He may never be fluent
in emotional language,
but he tries—
and that trying
is its own kind of love.
Sometimes healing
is just one sentence
spoken at the right time.

The Hallway Between my Brother and Me

In childhood,

our hallway was narrow

and always slightly too dim.

He paced it often,

lost in storms

I couldn't name then.

I stood at the end,

cracking jokes

or simply matching his silence.

I didn't know the words for support,

but I knew how to show up.

Even now,

as adults,

that invisible hallway remains—

a place where he knows

I will always be

if he needs me.

The Room Where I Finally Stepped into My Voice

The first time I presented professionally,
my body trembled
with old anxieties.
But when I looked at the parents in front of me,
their tired eyes,
their quiet hopes,
I knew why I was there.
My voice did not shake
because it had work to do.
Afterward,
I received a message from Santa Bob:
"Sunshine, you're changing lives."
And a call from my mother,
soft and warm:
"You're doing good things, mija."
In that moment,
I understood—
I wasn't just surviving my story.
I was using it
to light the path for others.

The Night Windows of My Mind

There are windows in my mind

that only open after midnight.

Ideas lean on the sill,

waiting to be acknowledged.

I no longer fear these openings.

I welcome them,

they are how I breathe.

Prayer Without a Name

My prayers are not spoken.

They rise from silence,

from breath,

from instinct.

Faith does not always need words

to be real.

The Bear on the Bed

He sits on the bed,

quiet witness to every version of me.

When I reach for him,

it is not regression.

It is remembrance,

a return to safety

I created for myself.

Grandfather's Conversations

I miss our conversations,

the ones we used to have

when life still felt steady

and I could sit beside you

without needing to explain myself.

There was a day I came home

with my hair tangled,

pulled by a boy at school

who thought hurting me was a joke.

My parents were upset,

imagining I had gotten into a fight,

but you—

you saw right through me.

You chuckled softly,

that little smirk tugging at your mouth,

and said,

"Te enojaste, ¿verdad?

But never let anyone,

especially a boy,

treat you that way, my dear."

You weren't mocking me.

You were teaching me.

You were reminding me

that my voice mattered

and that no one had the right

to make me feel small.

You didn't rush me.

You didn't talk over me.

You didn't minimize what I felt.

Instead,

you listened,

really listened,

like every word I spoke

deserved a place to land.

Our conversations were simple,

but they were anchors.

They shaped the way I saw myself,

the way I learned to stand tall,

the way I learned to say no
when something was wrong.
Even after grief came
and tried to blur the edges of memory,
your voice stayed clear.
Your humor stayed warm.
Your lessons stayed sharp.
I miss those conversations—
that sense of connection,
that quiet safety,
that feeling of being understood
without needing perfect words.
You may no longer be here,
but the way you listened
still guides me.
And the girl you believed in
is still becoming the woman
you hoped she would be.

From the Girl I Was

I was small

and my hair hurt

from where the boy had pulled it.

I walked home

trying not to cry

because I didn't want anyone to think

I had done something wrong.

When I told you,

you didn't get loud.

You didn't get angry at me.

You laughed a little

in that way you did

when you were both amused

and protective.

"Te enojaste, ¿verdad?"

you said,

and I nodded.

Then you told me,

calm and certain,

"Don't ever let anyone

treat you that way."

I didn't need big speeches.

I didn't need perfect comfort.

I just needed that moment—

your voice steady,

your presence warm,

your belief in me

stronger than the hurt I brought home.

Back then,

I didn't know the word for it.

But now I do.

It was love,

quiet and uncomplicated,

teaching me how to stand up

long before I learned how to explain

why I needed to.

My Father Learning How to Say My Name

He says my name
like a language he is still studying.
Not perfect,
but intentional,
and effort,
no matter how late,
still matters.

Five Years and a Hallway

Five years apart
felt like a decade.
But I stood guard,
quietly,
consistently,
in every hallway
life placed between us.

In Rooms Full of Small Talk

In rooms filled with surface words,
I feel like a book among flyers.
But when someone drops the mask
and speaks truth,
I breathe easier.
I was never made
for shallow water.

When I Step onto the Stage

My body trembles
then transforms.
Anxiety becomes energy.
Depth becomes clarity.
I speak,
not to impress,
but to translate
what others feel
but cannot say.

Blessing for the Men Who Stayed Kind

This is for the men

whose kindness was quiet

and sincere.

Their gentleness

did not fix me,

it simply reminded me

that kindness still exists.

Santa Bob: The Man Who Arrived Like A Season

I met him on a quiet afternoon,

over a simple lunch,

the kind where conversation moves easily

and nothing feels forced.

He listened more than he spoke,

nodding gently,

as if he understood

the kind of weight a person carries

when they are building something from scratch.

There was no grand reveal,

no sudden declaration of support.

Just a warmth in his presence,

a steadiness in his eyes,

a kindness that did not need to announce itself.

He was not dressed in the red coat that day.

No velvet hat.

Just a man with patience in his voice
and generosity tucked quietly
behind every word.
But something in him
felt like December,
a season that brings comfort
without asking anything in return.
After that lunch,
he stepped into my world
with a gentleness
I was not used to receiving
from men.
He supported Empathy in the Vines
as if it were his own vision.
He showed up early.
He stayed late.
He gave freely,
time, effort, gifts,
not for recognition,
but because he believed

in what the event was meant to provide

for our community.

And when he put on the Santa suit,

it didn't feel like a costume.

It felt like a continuation

of the kindness he already lived in.

He didn't ask for payment.

He didn't calculate what he gained.

He simply gave.

And gave.

And kept giving.

Later, long after the crowds were gone,

he would send a simple message:

"How are you, sunshine?"

or

"I'm proud of you. You did good."

Words I rarely heard

from the men in my life.

Words that landed softly

but stayed with me deeply.

He did not try to fill the role

of father or mentor.

He simply held space

in the way good people do,

quietly,

consistently,

with sincerity that doesn't need applause.

Santa Bob became a reminder

that sometimes support

does not come from where you expect,

and that kindness from a stranger

can feel like a miracle

when you are used to standing alone.

And maybe that is his magic,

not the suit,

not the beard,

not the holiday charm,

but the way he walks into people's lives

and leaves them warmer

than he found them.

Maria

Maria entered my life

without noise,

without ceremony,

without trying to impress.

She simply arrived

with presence.

The kind of presence

that steadies a room

without having to speak loudly.

She has a way of seeing people,

not the masks,

not the practiced smiles,

but the truth underneath.

Where others rush,

she observes.

Where others judge,

she understands.

Where others hesitate,

she steps forward.

Maria supported me

in ways I didn't know

I needed support.

Not with grand gestures,

not with dramatic acts,

but with the quiet gifts

that mean the most:

a message checking in,

a word of encouragement,

a reminder that I was not alone

in the work I was carrying.

She has this steadiness,

a calmness woven into her,

that makes people breathe easier

when she is near.

It reminds me

that strength doesn't always roar,

sometimes it stands beside you

in silence

and holds the moment steady.

Maria believed in me
before I remembered to believe in myself.
She saw what I was building
and treated it with dignity,
not as a favor,
not as an obligation,
but as something worthy
of her time and heart.
And in a world
where sincerity is rare
and motives are questioned,
her encouragement
felt like clean air.
Maria didn't need attention.
She didn't ask for recognition.
She simply showed up.
Fully.
Consistently.
Generously.
Not everyone carries
the kind of heart

that lifts others

with such ease.

But she does,

and she does it naturally.

Maria is proof

that some of the most important people

in our lives

are the ones who hold us up

without ever needing

to be seen doing it.

Closing Spell for My Own Heart

May I never apologize

for the way I feel the world.

May I trust my intuition.

May I release

every version of myself

I built for survival,

and keep only the ones

that feel like breathing.

The Woman Whose Love Holds the Walls Steady

There is a strength in my mother

that exists beyond language.

A presence that fills the room

even when she is silent.

She gives love

in the ways she knows,

through action,

through showing up,

through a loyalty

that does not shake

even under pressure.

We are similar

and sometimes that makes the air tense,

but it also makes the bond unbreakable.

No matter how my mood shifts,

or how her mind swirls,

I know she would cross oceans for me

without hesitation.

She is not perfect.

Neither am I.

But our love

is stronger than our misunderstandings.

Her heartbeat

is the first rhythm I ever learned,

and even now,

it reminds me

that I am never alone.

The Woman they Called Cabrona

They used to call my mother *cabrona*.
A word meant to sting,
to shame,
to mark her as "too much."
Too outspoken.
Too direct.
Too confident.
Too unwilling to bend
for anyone's comfort.
I remember the way women in the neighborhood said it
in low voices,
as if the sound of her strength
might echo back at them.
To them, *cabrona* meant trouble.
A woman who didn't stay in her place.
A woman who didn't bow her head.
A woman who didn't apologize
for taking up space.
But even as a child,
I saw the truth:

my mother wasn't a problem.
She was a force.
There was a day,
When my brother was seven,
when she marched into his school.
A teacher had dismissed him,
shrugged off my feelings
as if a child's truth was disposable.
My mother walked in
with steady steps
and eyes that didn't flinch.
She sat down,
looked that teacher straight in the face,
and said with a calm, cutting certainty,
"My son deserves respect."
No yelling.
No threats.
Just truth spoken
with the weight of a woman
who had survived far worse
than misunderstanding.
Later that night,
I heard her crying quietly,
not out of regret,

but because strength
always has a cost.
Women like her
are not handed gentleness.
They are expected to carry everything
and break nothing.
But here is what I understand now:
My mother did not earn the title *cabrona*.
She inherited it.
From women who crossed borders
with broken shoes,
who scrubbed floors to feed their families,
who were told to serve quietly
and never complain.
Cabrona was their armor.
Their shield.
Their badge of survival
in a world where soft women
did not make it far.
So when people called her that,
thinking they were insulting her,
they didn't realize
they were naming her strength.
Because she was the woman

who held our family together
when life split open.
The woman who stood up for us
even when her voice trembled afterward
in private.
The woman who trained me
to advocate without apology
because she never stepped aside
to make herself small.
Now, as an adult,
when I face systems that underestimate me,
when I fight for my children,
when I speak truth others avoid,
I feel her legacy in my spine.
If being a *cabrona*
means being brave,
being loyal,
being impossible to silence,
then I carry the title proudly.
She didn't raise me to be obedient.
She raised me to be resilient.
And I honor her
by refusing to shrink.

In Praise of The Cabrona

They called her *cabrona*
like it was a curse,
like it was something
to be whispered
behind closed doors.
But I saw the truth.
I saw the way she stood up
when others stayed quiet.
I saw the way she protected us
with eyes sharp as glass.
I saw the way she bent rules
that were never built for women like her
to survive.
They called her *cabrona*
because they feared a woman
who refused to break.
Because she didn't bow her head.

Because she didn't swallow her opinions.
Because she didn't let anyone
decide her worth.
I saw the power in it,
in the set of her jaw,
in the way she walked into a room
like she had already done the work
to earn her place.
And now,
I carry that same flame.
Not to start fires,
but to burn through lies.
Not to intimidate,
but to protect.
Not to dominate,
but to rise.
If strength makes me
a *cabrona,*
then let it be known,
I learned from the best.
Her courage
was my first inheritance.

Lita and Abu

I see my parents differently now,
not through the eyes of the child I was,
but through the eyes of the mother I became.
My children call her *Lita,*
a name that wraps itself
in affection and familiarity,
a name that softens her edges
and turns her into someone new.
They run into her arms
as if the world begins there,
as if she has always been
the safest place to land.
Her laugh is louder now,
her patience deeper,
her love more open
than I remember from childhood.
It's not that she wasn't loving then,
it's that life was heavier,
and survival took up space
where softness now lives.
And my father,

the man who once felt distant,
careful with emotion,
quiet in his affection,
becomes *Abu* the moment
my children enter the room.
He kneels to their height,
lets them climb him like a mountain,
lets their voices fill the silence
he once carried like a shield.
He smiles more now.
He holds them close
with warmth that feels new
and familiar all at once.
Sometimes I watch them
and feel my heart ache
in a way that is not painful
but full.
Full of gratitude,
full of understanding,
full of the healing
I didn't know I needed.
I realize now
that becoming grandparents
gave them permission
to love differently,
to be softer,

to be present,
to show tenderness
in ways they once guarded.
They are not the parents
I learned from as a child.
They are the grandparents
my children will remember,
open,
gentle,
devoted,
full of joy.
And watching them together
is like watching a second chance
unfold quietly in front of me.
Not to erase the past,
but to rewrite the future,
one embrace,
one laugh,
one whispered "Lita,"
one joyful "Abu,"
at a time.

Chapter 8: Final Thoughts

The Last Ember

I am the last ember

of a fire that refused to die,

glowing quietly

long after the flames

stopped reaching for the sky.

Not bright,

not loud,

but steady,

holding warmth

the world cannot name.

I learned the shape of myself

by walking through years

that tried to carve me hollow,

and still found room

to grow roots.

Not from guidance,

not from clarity,

but from grit.

From breath.

From a stubborn spark

that would not go out.

I became my own hearth.

My own shelter.

My own flame.

And if you are reading this,

holding these words like lanterns,

I want you to know:

you carry your own ember too.

even if it feels small.

even if you are the only one

who sees it.

you do not need to roar

to be alive.

you do not need to shine

like anyone else.

your glow is enough

to warm your hands

on the coldest nights,

to light the corner of a path

that belongs only to you.

protect it.

trust it.

let it burn

in its own language.

the world will try

to douse your flame

with expectations,

tilt your head this way,

speak softer,

be normal,

fit in.

but there is nothing normal

about surviving the dark

and turning it into your own fire.

you are the last ember.

and you are still burning.

The Bridge I Did Not Know I Was Building

For most of my life,

I walked as if the ground beneath me

might disappear at any moment.

Not because I lacked strength,

but because I had learned survival

without knowing it was survival.

I thought I was just moving,

one day into the next,

one challenge into another,

one chapter closing

only because I couldn't hold it open anymore.

But somewhere along the way,

without blueprint or permission,

I began building a bridge.

Not a straight bridge.

Not a polished one.

A bridge made from all the things

I didn't realize were shaping me,

from moments I mistook as failures,

from relationships that taught more by leaving

than staying,

from grief that carved its initials

into the quiet parts of me,

from victories so small

I almost missed them,

from growth that stretched

without asking first.

This bridge was not built

in the daylight.

It was built at strange hours,

in unexpected places:

in late-night kitchens,

in silent car rides,

in hospital waiting rooms,

in classrooms,

in therapy offices,

in whispered prayers,

in the exhausted breaths

between one responsibility and the next.

Every experience

was another plank.

Another nail.

Another length of rope.

And one day,

without fanfare,

I looked down and realized

I was no longer standing

where I began.

I had walked myself

to a different shore.

Not through certainty,

but through persistence.

Not through perfection,

but through movement.

Not through knowing the destination,

but through refusing to stop walking.

On this new shore,

I am not unfinished.

I am not lost.

I am not waiting for permission

to claim my place.

I am simply standing

exactly where I was always headed,

whether I knew it or not.

And when others arrive,

the ones who move differently,

feel deeply,

think in spirals,

carry invisible weights,

I will meet them on this bridge

I didn't know I was building.

And I will say:

"You made it.

You're here.

And you're not alone."

A Thank You to the Ones Like Me

thank you

for walking through these pages with me,

for opening the doors of your own mind

as I revealed the rooms inside mine.

thank you

for sitting with my words,

for breathing with them,

for letting them echo in places

you don't always show the world.

if you are autistic,

if you are neurodivergent,

if you have ever felt like a stranger

in your own body

or in your own family

or in the expectations of society,

I hope these poems reminded you

that you are not alone.

you are not strange.

you are not wrong.

you are not broken.

you simply do not fit

into a mold

that was never designed

with minds like ours in mind.

and that is not failure,

that is freedom.

your sensitivity is not a flaw.

your intensity is not a burden.

your quiet is not emptiness.

your depth is not danger.

your difference is not a defect.

your mind is a constellation

in a world that prefers straight lines,

and that makes you luminous

in ways others cannot imitate.

I hope these pages

gave you a place to land,

a moment of recognition,

a breath of relief,

a reminder that your inner world

is worthy of being understood

and honored.

and if you ever start to doubt yourself,

if the world feels too loud

or too sharp

or too demanding,

come back to these words

and remember:

there are others like you.

there are others like us.

we exist outside the mold,

and that is exactly

where brilliance lives.

thank you for being here.

thank you for being you.

may you walk forward

with the quiet certainty

that there is nothing wrong

with the way you are built.

and everything right

with the way you shine.

About the Author

Karla Luciana Chinen is a writer, advocate, educator, and autistic mother whose work centers on neurodivergence, identity, and the emotional landscapes that shape family life. She is the founder of Empathy for Autism California Inc, a nonprofit that offers support groups, parent trainings, community events, and education for families raising autistic children. Her lived experience, combined with her academic background in psychology and child development, guides her work with authenticity, clarity, and depth.

As a mother of two autistic children, she writes from within the reality she speaks about. Her storytelling reflects cultural roots, personal resilience, generational cycles, grief, love, and the lived moments that shape her understanding of disability and family systems. Her voice is emotionally intelligent, spiritually grounded, culturally aware, honest without harshness, and tender without fragility.

Outside of writing, she hosts "Voices Beyond the Spectrum," a bilingual podcast that amplifies stories from parents, professionals, and community members connected to autism and neurodivergence.

Karla lives in California, where she continues to write, advocate, and create safe, connected spaces where neurodivergent families feel seen, supported, and understood.

Made in the USA
Coppell, TX
10 February 2026

71719308R00115